India's Invisible Shackles

India's Invisible Shackles

Over 70,000 newspapers and more than 500 satellite news channels, does not always mean press freedom.

Shamim Zakaria

India's Invisible Shackles

Over 70,000 newspapers and more than 500 satellite news channels, does not always mean press freedom

Shamim Zakaria

About the Author

Shamim Zakaria is journalist, author and academic. Born and brought-up in the serene paradise of India's northeast, he did his schooling and spent most part of his early life in Guwahati before relocating to Delhi to pursue graduate study and thereafter to England for post-graduation. He holds a bachelor's degree with honours in Journalism and Mass Communication from India and a master's degree in International Journalism from the University of Sussex, UK.

A journalist at core of given calibre his writings are focused primarily on politics, human rights and other socio-political issues. His multitudinous articles have found place in a plethora of regional, national and international publications, disseminating in print and web-based medium. He has lived and worked internationally based out of England and China.

India's Invisible Shackles was initially an academic essay written during his post graduate study, which is now compiled into a book.

Get a closer glimpse of him and his work on:
www.shamimzakaria.com

Get in touch with the author:
mail@shamimzakaria.com

Join on the social media:
www.facebook.com/shamimzakariaofficial
www.twitter.com/shamimzakaria
www.instagram.com/shamim.zakaria

Table of Contents

Shamim Zakaria

Introduction

Considered to be the world's largest democracy though freedom of press is guaranteed in the Indian constitution, but the state time and again tries to exercise its control over the autonomy of press. This book tries to explore why the existence of over 70,000 newspapers and more than 500 satellite channels in India, does not necessarily mean having enough journalistic freedom. It discusses how in India despite of not having any censorship laws, the government uses various tools and mechanism to curb journalists' freedom. To explain this further various case studies have been done and newspaper reports including freedom of press index from reliable websites have been quoted.

Numerous newspaper reports and footage of various television interviews have been analyzed to elicit the tug of war between journalists and the state. Light has also been thrown on how editors and owners of newspapers acting at the behest of the state compel journalists to kill their explosive and investigative stories which are often critical of the establishment.

Starting with the ideals of journalism and its role in a democracy the various chapters also explain why curbing freedom of press and restraining journalists from freely and fairly reporting stories, causes the fabric of democracy to unstitch.

The state of press freedom in China has also been briefly explained as a juxtaposition to emphasize on how China being a democratic dictatorship under an authoritarian government directly censors the press. On the other hand, India being a democracy tries controlling the press indirectly in a concealed manner, giving rise to the phenomenon of 'invisible censorship'. Furthermore, espying the state of journalism in China will also give a deeper understanding of censorship and the various underlying questions around it.

Journalism and its Role in Democracy

For some journalism is a mere profession with sheer adventure along with perks of traveling to remotest locations and strife torn zones, while for certain people journalism is perhaps a profession of compulsive storytelling. While according to many, journalism is bearing the flag of being the voice of the mass.

However, surprisingly researchers apparently are of the opinion that there cannot be an absolute definition of journalism. According to John Russial, Peter Laufer and Janet Wasko, having a formal definition of journalism might invite problems for an organization, as a strict definition could be used in court against the organisation when it deviates from the parameters of journalism that has been set (Russial, Laufer, Wasko, 299).

Perhaps that is one reason why research about journalism among journalists has been established as a widely acknowledged field, particularly in the second half of the 20th century (Deuze, 442). In fact, Deuze in 'What is Journalism?' suggests that worldwide one can find universities, schools and colleges with dedicated departments, research and teaching programs in journalism and this field even has its own international and national journals (Deuze, 442).

What the article 'Journalism in Crisis' suggests is though journalism cannot have a definition but it is news that can be defined. It states that news can be defined as anything that changes the status quo and gets reported (Russial, Laufer, Wasko, 300).

With journalism comes its role in a democracy. Deuze believes that to delineate the role of journalism it is important to define journalism as an ideology. Doing so primarily means understanding journalism in terms of how journalists give meaning to their news-work (Deuze, 443). Ideology more aptly is a system of beliefs or characteristic of a particular group, including – but not limited to – the general process of the production of meanings and ideas (within that group) (Deuze, 445).

The second important thing why defining journalism as an ideology helps to understand it more is because according to popular believe of media scholars journalists' professionalization is process of ideological development, emerging from an ideology served to continuously refine and reproduce a consensus about who was a 'real' journalist, and what (parts of) news media at any time would be considered examples of 'real' journalism (Deuze, 444). The following are Deuze's journalistic ideals.

The first such ideal of journalism according to Deuze is, journalism is a public service and journalists are working as some kind of representative watchdog of the status quo in the name of people, who are indirectly paying for the service by means of purchasing newspapers, watching or listening news that is being broadcast or clicking on the news sites (Deuze, 447). What he calls journalists as the ones disseminating the information and public as consumers who are receiving the news.

Objectivity and neutrality has been stated as another most important trait of journalists by Deuze. Although objectivity has a problematic status in current thinking about the impossibility of value-neutrality, academics and journalists alike revisit this value through synonymous concepts like 'fairness', 'professional distance', 'detachment' or 'impartiality' to define and (re-)legitimize what media practitioners do (Deuze, 448). Although there have been numerous contradictions and debates around being objective however the bottom line in the words of Deuze is that the embrace, rejection as well as critical reappraisal of objectivity all help to keep it alive as an ideological cornerstone of journalism (Deuze, 448).

The second important journalistic ideal elicited by Deuze is journalists enjoying editorial autonomy and having the freedom to report. The reason as specified in 'What is journalism?' is, reporters across the globe feel that their work can only thrive and flourish in a society that protects its media from censorship; in a company that saves its journalists from the marketers; in a newsroom where journalists are not merely the lackeys of their editors; and at a desk where a journalist is adequately supported through further training and education (Deuze, 448).

Having a sense of immediacy among the journalists is Deuze's another journalistic ideal. As the popular saying goes 'today's news is tomorrow's history, perhaps that is the reason for journalists to be working in an aura of instantaneity and immediatism, as 'news' stresses the novelty of information as its defining principle (Deuze, 449). Therefore, work of journalists involves notions of speed, fast decision-making, hastiness, and working in accelerated real-time (Deuze, 449). Surveys has revealed how journalists are subjected to pressurizing environment as novices and as per scholars doing so propels journalists to work in a 'non-stop' 24/7-digital environment in due course of time(Deuze,449). The last and the most talked about ideals of journalism is ethics. Debates, discussions and perhaps research around ethical segment of journalism has been a never ending one.

Numerous organizations have laid their own set of ethical guidelines, which more or less speaks of adhering to the same professional standard. The BBC too has published their own set of guide lines which they call journalistic 'values.' However, surprisingly journalists worldwide disagree on whether a code of ethical conduct should be in place or not, they do share a sense of being ethical – which in turn legitimizes journalists' claims to the position as (free and fair) watchdogs of society (Deuze, 449).

Apart from the above stated ideals few of the other roles of journalism may include, serving the political system by providing information, discussion and debate on public affairs, enlightening the public, safeguarding rights of an individual, maintaining its own self sufficiency (Siebert, Fred S, 1956).

However, there have been contradicting views as well to the above stated ideals of journalism and 'objectivity' has been at the centre of this never ending discussion. Eminent Indian journalist Abhinandan Shekhri during a Tedx (2015) talk stressed on the argument that there is no such thing called objectivity. He states that even in the field of science there cannot be anything as objective as according to scientists, the outcome depends on what experiment we conduct (00:04:13 - 00:04:20). According to Abhinandan there cannot be anything as objective news, there can be only fair and transparent news (Tedx, 2015, 00:04:31 – 00:04:38).

Understanding Press Censorship Through China

C ensorship in a broader sense and as the dictionary defines, it is trying to curb speech, public communication or dissemination of other information by the establishment primarily because it believes that the information imparted may be objectionable, harmful, sensitive, politically incorrect or inconvenient. The ones acting as gatekeeper between the sender and the receiver are governments, media outlets, authorities or other groups or institutions in power to supress.

Press censorship was mostly prevalent during the early war times when information was being withheld from disseminating in order to protect national security of a nation and safeguard pubic morale from the corrosion of enemy propaganda (Eggleston, 313). The tactics as Eggleston mentions in 'Press Censorship' might be putting a ban on broadcast of certain news or forbidding from covering certain issues or even a control over the various communication mediums like radio, newspaper, television and telegraph (Eggleston, 313).

For an in-depth understanding of censorship in journalism, types and its implications we take the example of China. Over the years censorship in China has certainly been a point of great interest for media researchers and scholars.

Starting with the online arena. Going by numbers, to comply with the government, each individual site privately employs up to 1,000 censors (King, Pan,

Roberts, 326). As compiled in the journal American Political Science review (2013), approximately 20,000–50,000 Internet police and Internet monitors as well as an estimated 250,000–300,000 "50 cent party members" at all levels of government—central, provincial, and local—participate in this huge effort (p 327). China overall is tied with Burma at 187th of 197 countries on a scale of press freedom, but the Chinese censorship effort is by far the largest (King, Pan, Roberts, 327).

Censorship on freedom to speak exists in all forms of media. Protection over the web space seems very much interesting. There are three primary ways of doing so, the first one is "The Great Firewall of China" that completely bans certain website from operating in the country (King, Pan, Roberts, 327). The other two ways according to the author are 'keyword blocking,' which abstains the user from posting certain words or phrases which are being banned. The third and the last one is when after content is posted on the web, the censors read and remove those they find objectionable (King, Pan, Roberts, 327).

Focusing specifically on journalism self-censorship is the most commonly used form of controlling content. Given the political setup of China, journalist prefer this mechanism to crop content because it minimises political risk (Tong, 593). Another important advantage of this is it helps the newsroom bypass the political 'minefields' and makes sure politically sensitive reports get published (Tong, 594). In this self-censoring environment the original reports are sent by the journalist to the editors who takes the final call on if it would find a place in the publication or how it should be published based on the position of the media outlet, underlying ideology and socio-political situation (Tong, 594).

The government has a stringent control over the news arena, which prohibit the media from reporting on issues which might poses a threat to the national stability (Tong, 595). As explained by Tong (2009) the other topics that cannot be reported are criticism of the Party leaders, riots and human rights abuse and severe accidents and disasters. These topics which may be enlisted as the pre-publication restrictions where instructions on what should be reported and what not are imparted beforehand. But the authorities also take to post publication censorship where if the media organisations violate the guidelines, warnings are issued to the newsrooms which may often lead to political crackdowns on those media (Tong, 595). The Propaganda Department spearheads this media censorship, journalists flouting the 'propaganda disciplines' often leads to imprisonment, complete closure of the organisation and reorganisation of the media outlets (Thomas, Zaharom, 180).

Furthermore, since television journalism began in China it has been used by the government as a propaganda tool tasked at 'propagate politics', 'disseminate knowledge' and 'enrich the lives of the masses' with each and every news program serving as an ideological compass (Chang, Ren, 14). Throwing light on the most popular China Central Television (CCTV), it is the most tightly controlled television outlet in the country with regular monitoring of the content by Party elders (Thomas, Zaharom, 183).

Shamim Zakaria

Implications of Press Censorship on Democracy

Democracy and journalism are very much complimentary to each other and perhaps that's the reason why journalism is always termed as the fourth estate of democracy. The path journalism and democracy took, and the role journalism played in this development, have shaped the journalistic ethos (Josephi, 475). Josephi in the article 'How much democracy does journalism need?' (2012) points out journalism as synonym for democracy and that there can be no journalism without democracy and vice-versa.

For instance, in the Soviet Union too there was the existence of media since there existed communication but there was no journalism because there was no democracy (Josephi, 475).

This very much makes evident the importance of journalism in a democracy and censorship or control over the press certainly misbalances the core values of democracy that includes promoting values such as equality, social harmony, the legal framework for freedom of speech among others (Josephi, 479).

The first among the ill effects of press censorship on democracy is lack of a collective opinion among the mass. Restraining the formation of a collective opinion in democracy is another ill effect of press censorship. This has been very much evident in the case of China. Curbing freedom of speech and expression reduces the probability of collective action by clipping social ties whenever any collective movements are in evidence or expected (King, Pan, Roberts, 326). Furthermore, having censorship also possesses great challenge for researchers studying various socio-political issues, because information available in the public domain are only from one source that is the government. Available information though answers important questions, but in gauging government intent, they are widely known to be indirect and often of dubious nature and offers a view of government interests thus appraising only one side of the story (King, Pan, Roberts, 327).

For journalists working in such kind of an environment greatest difficulty is finding voices from members of public to speak on sensitive and political stories. When people have the information that are sought by reporters they may not be willing to express themselves freely (King, Pan, Roberts, 327). Also journalists when working under censorship are in a lack of professional and personal security. In has been observed that reporters in China who try pushing the barriers of censorship tend to have a short professional life primarily due to the high pressured work environments they endure and the severe censorship imposed on their reporting (Shen, Zhang, 374). There's also a threat to their personal life because not adhering to the guidelines provided by the government may land them up in prison.

As democracy is all about collective voice of all sections of the society and press plays a key role by participating in formation of a collective opinion (Shen, Zhang, 375). With control over the press, it ends up only serving the interest of the country's political and economic elites thus supressing the marginalised and alternative voices of the nation (Thomas, Zaharom, 179).

Lastly but not least, press censorship kills the ethos of journalism. With control over journalism the very professional values - neutrality and participant, disseminating information to the public with an endeavour at social reform becomes obscure (Shen, Zhang, 375). This is because the establishment with its control over press, the objective of journalism shifts from raising people's concern to promoting the legitimacy of the government (Thomas, Zaharom, 181).

Shamim Zakaria

Questions Around Journalistic Freedom in India

Considered to be one of the largest democracies in the world the freedom of speech and expression has been enshrined in the very constitution of India. Article 19 of the Indian constitution affirms that all citizens shall have the right to freedom of speech and expression along with various other rights pertaining to exercise of freedom.

Perhaps that's what makes India home to more than 70,000 newspapers and over 500 satellite channels in several languages (BBC, 2012). However, despite such robust growth of media in the country, according to the 2016 Reporters without Border, Freedom of Press Index, India stands at 133 out of 180 countries. In terms of the colour category map it is assigned as red color which indicates 'very bad' state of press freedom. Despite its status as the world's largest democracy, the extent of India's freedom of expression remains a controversial topic (The World Street Journal, 2012). Surprisingly though there is a variation in the rankings but India in accordance to the colour category stands in the same position as Bangladesh, Pakistan, Turkey and Iraq – countries that are facing sharp challenges when it comes to freedom of press.

India's Invisible Shackles

The data of further elicits-

Journalists and bloggers are attacked and anathematized by various religious groups that are quick to take offence. At the same time, it is hard for journalists to cover regions such as Kashmir that are regarded as sensitive by the government. Prime Minister Narendra Modi seems indifferent to these threats and problems, and there is no mechanism for protecting journalists. Instead, in a desire to increase control of media coverage, Modi envisages opening a journalism university run by former propaganda ministry officials (RSF, 2016).

While the government has not openly exercised direct control over the press however time and again it has been observed that the state through various other machineries has indirectly attempted at curbing the freedom of press. This could be trailed to the existence of what we might call an 'invisible press censorship' in India.

Three newspapers published from Nagaland – a state on the hilly terrain of India's northeastern region on November 16, 2016 decided to publish the newspaper keeping their editorial pages blank. The reason behind this was that The Assam Rifles – a wing of India's paramilitary force in October 2016 had told editors to stop covering rebel group National Socialist Council of Nagaland - Khaplang (BBC, 2015). Nagaland has been an insurgent prone zone since long where rebels have been fighting for an independent homeland for more than 60 years in a bitter battle against Indian security forces. Often the press is caught in between this tug of war because they decide on publishing both sides of the story and that is a reason why newspapers in Nagaland face accusations from security forces of taking sides (BBC, 2015). The editors of the Morung Express, the Eastern Mirror and the Nagaland Page was quoted in BBC saying they were protesting against the diktat from paramilitary force.

This has been a very common mechanism of the state where it often tries to control the journalists on the pretext of law and order situation.

There has also been direct intimidation to journalists who are critical of the authorities. Malini Subramaniam a senior journalist who had extensively reported on human rights violations and police atrocities, allegations of sexual violence by security forces and fake encounters in Bastar region, was forced to pack up from the region following alleged intimidation by Bastar police and a self-styled anti-Maoist group (Hindustan Times, 2016). Bastar is considered to be India's red corridor with the banned outfit Communist Party of India-Maoist fighting guerilla war to acquire their rights.

Interestingly the police took two days to lodge Malini's complaint and on the other hand police wrote a letter to Malini's landlord and summoned him to the police station leading to unwarranted harassment (Hindustan Times, 2016).

Journalists were also being targeted by police who were covering the Jawaharlal Nehru University row. The President of the university's students' union was arrested on February 2016 on charges of sedition for allegedly being involved in anti-national sloganeering during a protest demonstration (The Indian Express, 2016). Family member of Manas Roshan, a 26-year-old reporter working for the New Delhi Television channel was harassed by Delhi police for the channels critical coverage of authorities (Scroll, 2016). Three policemen in plain clothes arrived at the reporter's home and threatened his brother on pretext of investigation as the police believed that Manas was in touch with the JNU students who were absconding (Scroll, 2016).

While it is a part of journalist's job to be in touch with various people involved in story and also anonymous sources, but this seemed to be beyond the understanding of the authorities. Such acts of police irked the media fraternity at large including senior journalists. Sanjoy Narayan editor of 'Hindustan Times' maintained that journalists should not be the subject of police questioning over stories they are reporting (Scroll, 2016). According to him drawing journalists into the investigative processes of the police threatens independence of the press and hinders the ability to serve public interest (Scroll, 2016).

Back in 2001 with his sting operation journalist Mathew Samuel exposed a high profile bribery scandal in India's defense ministry that saw the involvement of bureaucrats, politicians and generals of the India army (The New York Times, 2001). This resulted in resignation of the then India's powerful defense minister, George Fernandes and also led to arrest of top notch officials. However, later on the journalist was arrested under the Official Secret Act and charged with snooping and espionage for intruding and disseminating sensitive information related to the country's security (Outlook, 2012). Mathew was eventually acquitted of all the charges in 2016, but it took him 15 years of court battle to prove his innocence (Tehelka, 2016).

Apart from these incidents, previously there has been continuing violation of human rights in Chhattisgarh where journalists, critical of the police and the state, have been regularly harassed and has also led to arrests of journalists.

In the year 1991-92 a journalist Premraj reporting from this same Bastar, was booked under the Terrorist and Disruptive Activity (Prevention) Act (TADA). He was charged with being close to the Maoists but was later acquitted by the courts due to dearth of evidence (Outlook Magazine, 2016).

As of recently on March this year Deepak Jaiswal, a young reporter of a vernacular newspaper based in Dantewada district of Bastar , was arrested in a case of "entering the examination hall, trespassing, obstructing public servant in discharge of public function" (The Hindu, 2016).

News reports published in The Hindu informed that, Mr. Jaiswal was a close associate of journalist Prabhat Singh, another journalist who was arrested by the police earlier on March 2016. Mr. Jaiswal was nabbed from court premises in Dantewada, where he had gone to witness court proceedings in Mr. Singh's case (The Hindu, 2016).

There have also been numerous instances of physical violence incited by police on the journalists. Back in 2012 Azhar Qadri, a Srinagar-based journalist with 'The Tribune' was ruthlessly beaten up by an Indian Police Service officer and detained for more than an hour at a police station while the former was covering a student protest in the city (The Tribune, 2013).

Furthermore, there has been allegations on police for murder of journalists as well. Shahjahanpur based journalist, Jagendra Singh died from burn injuries on June 2015. Apart from being a freelance journalist he was very active on social media and his Facebook page became source of information for several local scribes for getting story cues (The Indian Express, 2015). In his dying declaration the journalist claimed that he was burnt by the local police at the behest of Minister Ram Murti Verma since Jagendra was constantly reporting about the minister's involvement in unlawful activities, including forced land occupation and illegal mining (The Hindu, 2015).

Apart from the indirect means of controlling the press there has been also direct clampdown on journalism, though it is only the foreign press mostly on the radar.

The Al Jazeera English Channel was banned for five days in India for its reporting on the controversial Kashmir region (Al Jazeera, 2015). The channel was taken off-air due to its report that concerned maps which on occasions during 2013 and 2014 did not mark Pakistan-controlled Kashmir as a separate territory (Al Jazeera, 2015).

A 1990 report published in The New York Times explained at length about India government's crackdown on both foreign and Indian journalists from reporting about the turbulent the Kashmir Valley. The report further mentioned about reporters being detained at hotels and then expelled from the Valley, the Muslim-dominated northern part of Jammu and Kashmir State (The New York Times, 1990).

During the same year a shipment of the Far East Economic Review 1990 Yearbook was seized, apparently because a map in it depicted the Jammu and Kashmir as an area in dispute between India and Pakistan and also because it reflected lost promises of India and Pakistan in 1948 and 1949 to hold a plebiscite in the valley that is yet to be fulfilled (The New York Times, 1990).

Back in 2008 visa applications of Swedish journalists Ulrika Nandra and foreign correspondent of Swedish daily Göteborgs-Posten and Marina Malmgren, were rejected by Indian authorities. The decision came in aftermath of the critical articles they wrote about social problems prevailing India, according to Swedish radio programme, 'The Media' (Business Standard, 2015). After filing her visa application when she did not get any response from the concerned authorities, representatives of the media for which Nandra worked, held a meeting with the Indian embassy in February 2008 in which the embassy said they were displeased with her reports, including one about sex trafficking in Mumbai and a series of articles about changing gender roles in India (Business Standard, 2015).

Also at times the state might use its various laws against journalists or anyone who according to the state is acting against the government. On August last year the state government of Maharashtra issued a circular to the police which entitled the police with powers to initiate actions against those critical of the state or central government (Economic Times, 2015).

Sedition has been one of the most commonly used laws in India to hound journalists and activists. The law and its use has always been a point of fierce debate. This law was introduced in India in 1870 during the British colonial regime to suppress India's freedom movement and since then the law is prevalent in the country (The Times of India, 2016).
Back in 2012 journalist and cartoonist Aseem Trivedi was arrested and tried under sedition for drawing and writing satirical pieces against the Indian parliament. He also ardently raised his voice against corruption through his website 'cartoons against corruption' which was suspended by the police (The Wall Street Journal, 2012)

The Amnesty International has time and again called for scrapping of the sedition laws. They are of the opinion that in healthy democracies there can be no place for draconian laws such as sedition that is slapped on people merely for questioning the government (The Time of India, 2016).

Censorship might also exist inside newsrooms where journalists are not given enough freedom to report and file stories, thus curbing the editorial freedom. Rahul Pandita the erstwhile Opinion and Special Stories Editor of 'The Hindu' newspaper, resigned in 2015 due to differences with the paper's editor (Firstpost, 2015). In his resignation letter he mentioned about not given enough freedom by the senor editors.

Stories are also seen being killed by editors due to political pressures. Back in 2005 veteran journalist and former executive editor of 'Tehelka' magazine Vijay Simha did an exclusive interview with Indian politician Rahul Gandhi. Simha was the first ever journalist to interview this top politician. Rahul Gandhi at that time being a novice in politics spoke his heart out giving many explosive answers about his party (Zee News, 00:00:44 – 00:01:00). This irked many of the senior party leaders who started pressurizing the editor of Tehelka magazine, Tarun Tejpal to stop the story from getting published (Zee News, 00:01:02 – 00:01:23) Thus, at the end the story suffered due to political pressure.

Another young journalist working for one of India's topnotch news channels, Zee News resigned this year on ethical grounds. Vishwa Deepak, the journalist in his resignation letter made it public that the channel was deliberately misinterpreting a story to serve interest of a certain political group (Hindustan Times, 2016).

Senior editors, owners and publishers dictating the content of the newspaper and not allowing enough editorial freedom often acts as another form of invisible press censorship. This makes the journalists stand in the middle of a battle and put up a fight that will eventually serve no purpose for anyone. When senior journalist and the then Resident editor of The Hindu, Praveen Swami quit the paper in 2014 citing editorial freedom, he stated that working in such kind of an environment feels like working for Pol Pot, who was at the helm of one of the most brutal, radical regimes in Cambodia (Firstpost, 2014).

Conclusion

After examining the incidents that pose questions around journalists' freedom and autonomy in India and also briefly analyzing the journalism scenario in China, it can be concluded that all forms of state tries to control the press. Though the level of control and intensity might vary but no state can tolerate journalists being critical of the government.

While in China the press is being officially regulated by the propaganda department that lays down various editorial guidelines compelling the journalists to crop their reporting and self-censor news reports, in India no such direct law of press regulation exists. However, state clamps censorship on the press by using its various laws primarily Law of Sedition, Official Secret Act, charges of espionage etc. Unwarranted harassment, detention and intimidating journalists by using police and administration can also be seen as a tool to curb freedom of press.

Focusing on foreign journalist, government of India banning foreign publication and not granting visas to foreign correspondents because the reports were critical of the establishment can also be seen as a form of press censorship. The Indian government, unlike its Chinese counterpart is democratically elected and governed by the Constitution. It certainly cannot have a policy that demands positive news – and that too from foreign journalists.

Editors succumbing to political pressures and in turn asking their reporters to change the story angle or stories being completely halted from publication is a kind of censorship encompassing newsrooms thus inducing a form of self-censorship or rather invisible self-censorship. Threat to press freedom is always a slow poisoning for a democracy that endangers the freedoms guaranteed to the press and put at risk the sovereignty of the citizens (Gupta, 300). The state exercising its control over journalism will further diminish the role of the press in interest of the public and shrink opportunities to connect with people and ideas (Gupta, 300).

Bibliography

Russial, John, Peter Laufer, and Janet Wasko. "Journalism in Crisis?" *Javnost - The Public* 22.4 (2015): 299-312. Web.

Deuze, M. "What Is Journalism?: Professional Identity and Ideology of Journalists Reconsidered." *Journalism* 6.4 (2005): 442-64. Web.

Siebert, Fred S. *Four Theories of the Press: The Authoritarian, Libertarian, Social Responsibility, and Soviet Communist Concepts of What the Press Should Be and Do.* Urbana: U of Illinois, 1956. Print.

Eggleston, Wilfrid. *Press Censorship; an Address Delivered at Kingston, before the Canadian Political Science Association, on May 23rd, 1941.* Place of Publication Not Identified, 1941. Print.

King, Gary, Jennifer Pan, and Margaret E. Roberts. "How Censorship in China Allows Government Criticism but Silences

Collective Expression." *Am Polit Sci Rev American Political Science Review* 107.02 (2013): 326-43. Web.

Tedx Talks. *Youtube.* Web. 25 Apr. 2016. <https://www.youtube.com/watch?v=jY9nAdhAO1E>. Journalism of Independence | Abhinandan Sekhri | TEDxJaiHindCollege

Tong, J. "Press Self-censorship in China: A Case Study in the Transformation of Discourse." *Discourse & Society* 20.5 (2009): 593-612. Web.

Chang, Jiang, and Hailong Ren. "Television News as Political Ritual: Xinwen Lianbo and China's Journalism Reform within the Party-state's Orbit." *Journal of Contemporary China* 25.97 (2015): 14-24. Web.

Thomas, Pradip, and Zaharom Nain. "The State, Market, and Media Control in China." *Who Owns the Media?: Global Trends and Local Resistances*. London: Zed, 2004. Print.

Josephi, B. "How Much Democracy Does Journalism Need?" *Journalism* 14.4 (2012): 474-89. Web.

Shen, Fei, and Zhi'an Zhang. "Who Are the Investigative Journalists in China? Findings from a Survey in 2010." Chinese Journal of Communication 6.3 (2013): 374-84. Web.

Soutik Biswas. "Why Are India's Media under Fire?" BBC. 12 Jan. 2012. Web. 3 May 2016. <http://www.bbc.co.uk/news/world-asia-india-16524711>.

"Government Indifference to Threats against Journalists." Reporters without Borders. 2016. Web. 3 May 2016. <https://rsf.org/en/india>.

Vikas Pandey. "Blank Space: Why Nagaland Papers Ran Empty Editorials." BBC. 17 Nov. 2015. Web. 3 May 2016. <http://www.bbc.co.uk/news/world-asia-india-34841210>.

Ejaz Kaisar. "Attacked, Intimidated, Bastar Journo Malini Subramaniam Packs up." Hindustan Times. 20 Feb. 2016. Web. 3 May 2016. <http://www.hindustantimes.com/india/anti-maoist-group-bastar-police-compel-journalist-to-leave-jagdalpur/story-EIOsLGMc7FclyQg7JmeFiP.html>.

Prakash Dubey, Seema Chisti, and Vinod Verma. "Challenges To Journalism In Bastar." Outlook. 29 Mar. 2016. Web. 3 May 2016. <http://www.outlookindia.com/website/story/challenges-to-journalism-in-bastar/296781>.

Pavan Dahat. "Another Journalist Arrested in Bastar." The Hindu. 26 Mar. 2016. Web. 3 May 2016. <http://www.thehindu.com/news/national/other-states/another-journalist-arrested-in-bastar-journalist-association-blocks-police-naxal-coverage-in-protest/article8399853.ece>.

"Human Rights Commission Seeks Statement of Facts from Journalist." The Tribune. 31 Aug. 2013. Web. 3 May 2016. <http://www.tribuneindia.com/2013/20130901/kashmir.htm#8>.

Aneesha Mathur. "JNU Row: Kanhaiya Kumar Gets Bail and a Lesson on Thoughts That 'infect... (like) Gangrene'." The Indian Express. 3 Mar. 2016. Web. 3 May 2016. <http://indianexpress.com/article/india/india-news-india/kanhaiya-kumar-bail-jnu-delhi-high-court/>.

Supriya Sharma, and Rohan Venkataramakrishnan. "'Insidious Intimidation': Delhi Police Knock on the Doors of Journalists Covering the JNU Row." Scroll. 22 Feb. 2016. Web. 3 May 2016.

<http://scroll.in/article/803975/insidious-intimidation-delhi-police-visit-homes-of-journalists-covering-the-jnu-row>.

Manish Shahu. "Journalist's Facebook Page Was Source of Stories for Others to Pick." The Indian Express. 12 June 2015. Web. 3 May 2016. <http://indianexpress.com/article/cities/lucknow/journalists-facebook-page-was-source-of-stories-for-others-to-pick/>.

Mohammad Ali. "In a U-turn, 'sole Witness' Says Social Media Journalist Committed Self-immolation." The Hindu. 18 June 2015. Web. 3 May 2016. <http://www.thehindu.com/news/national/other-states/up-journalist-jagendra-singh-death-main-witness-statement/article7329247.ece>.

Barbara Crossette. "India Barring Foreign Journalists From Turbulent Kashmir." The New York Times. 18 Feb. 1990. Web. 4 May 2016. <http://www.nytimes.com/1990/02/18/world/india-barring-foreign-journalists-from-turbulent-kashmir.html>.

"Why Certain Foreign Journalists Are Barred from Entering India." Boom Live, 24 Oct. 2015. Web. 4 May 2016. <http://www.business-standard.com/article/current-affairs/why-certain-foreign-journalists-are-barred-from-entering-india-115102400386_1.html>.

"Criticising Government Can Be Sedition in Maharashtra Now." Economic Times. Bennett, Coleman & Co. Ltd., 5 Sept. 2015. Web. 4 May 2016. <http://articles.economictimes.indiatimes.com/2015-09-05/news/66241363_1_sedition-aseem-trivedi-maharashtra-government>.

"When Governments Used Sedition Law." The Times of India. Bennett, Coleman & Co. Ltd., 16 Feb. 2016. Web. 4 May 2016.

Preetika Rana. "Cartoonist Faces Ban on Right to Poke Fun." The Wall Street Journal. 4 Jan. 2012. Web. 16 May 2016. <http://blogs.wsj.com/indiarealtime/2012/01/04/cartoonist-faces-ban-on-right-to-poke-fun/>.

Subhabrata Guha. "Respect Dissent, Scrap Law on Sedition, Says Amnesty." The Times of India. Bennett, Coleman & Co. Ltd., 27 Apr. 2016. Web. 16 May 2016.

"Rahul Pandita's Resignation Letter to The Hindu's Malini Parthasarthy Goes Viral." Firstpost. 2 Jan. 2015. Web. 16 May 2016. <http://www.firstpost.com/living/rahul-panditas-resignation-letter-to-the-hindus-malini-parthasarthy-goes-viral-2026605.html>.

"Journalist Resigns from News Channel over JNU Coverage." Hindustan Times. HT Media Ltd., 22 Feb. 2016. Web. 16 May 2016.

Gupta, Smita. "Post-liberalisation India: How Free Is the Media?" South Asia: Journal of South Asian Studies 28.2 (2005): 283-300. Web. 18 May 2016.

"Vijay Simha Tells Zee Media How Tarun Tejpal Killed a Story on Rahul Gandhi." Interview by Dilip Tiwari. Zee News. 2 Dec. 2013. Web. 18 May 2016.

Dugger, Celia W. "The Sting That Has India Writhing." The New York Times. 16 Mar. 2001. Web. 18 May 2016.

Mathew Samuel. "After Eleven Years, It Stings To Say This..." Outlook. 12 Mar. 2012. Web. 18 May 2016.

"Breather for Former Tehelka Editor Mathew Samuel in Operation WestEnd Case." Tehelka. Alchemist Media, 19 Feb. 2016. Web. 18 May 2016.

<http://www.tehelka.com/2016/02/breather-for-former-tehelka-editor-mathew-samuel-in-operation-westend-case/>.